MANAGING YOUR
MONEY AND FINANCES™

Getting Your First Job

Xina M. Uhl and Daniel E. Harmon

Rosen
YA™

New York

Published in 2020 by The Rosen Publishing Group, Inc.
29 East 21st Street, New York, NY 10010

Library of Congress Cataloging-in-Publication Data

Names: Uhl, Xina M., author. | Harmon, Daniel E., author.
Title: Getting your first job / Xina M. Uhl and Daniel E. Harmon.
Description: First edition. | New York : Rosen Publishing,
2020. | Series: Managing your money and finances |
Includes bibliographical references and index.
Identifiers: LCCN 2018048118| ISBN 9781508188438
(library bound) | ISBN 9781508188421 (pbk.)
Subjects: LCSH: Teenagers—Employment—
Juvenile literature. | Income—Juvenile literature.
| Finance, Personal—Juvenile literature.
Classification: LCC HD6270 .U265 2020
| DDC 650.140835—dc23
LC record available at https://lccn.loc.gov/2018048118

Manufactured in the United States of America

CONTENTS

INTRODUCTION

Work is one of the best ways teens and adults have of earning an income. Not only does a first job provide money for needs and wants, but it also provides a helpful learning experience for future work that may be more in line with your skills, talents, and likes. This learning experience also provides you with an excellent opportunity for you to manage money. In fact, you quickly see that money management is not just a good idea; it's a requirement for a life in which you can meet short- and long-term goals without compromising your enjoyment of life.

As a young person, you may receive most of your money from your parents. Perhaps you receive a weekly allowance. When you work for money, though, you have a new appreciation for how much effort and time it takes to earn a wage. If you remember how much work went into each paycheck, you will understand why it is important not to waste your hard-earned money.

Young people who live at home with their parents may dream of all the things they want to buy: entertainment, new technology, the latest fashions. While some teens look for odd jobs to earn money for special wants or occasions, like a summer trip, new car, or college, others must work to help support their families. Some teens may already know what kind of career they want to have in the future, and they look for a job that will provide experience in that industry.

Odd jobs, like making crafts to sell online, babysitting, mowing yards, walking dogs, or tutoring, can provide some income for young people. But many teenagers begin to look for regular jobs as they reach the minimum employment age in their states.

Retail businesses provide most jobs available to teens. McDonald's, Wendy's, Jack-in-the-Box, and other chain restaurants hire teens to be cashiers and cooks. Supermarkets and other stores need employees to bag groceries and stock shelves. Most of these jobs pay minimum wage or slightly higher. Adults have a hard time making ends meet at minimum wage. If you do not need to pay for living expenses, like rent, utilities, and food, you may just want spending money for fun. By establishing the good habits of budgeting, saving, and even investing, you will find it much easier to meet future goals and make your money work for you instead of always living paycheck to paycheck.

A first job provides more than money; it also provides a sense of worth. By listening carefully to a supervisor's instructions and watching other, more established, employees at work, you can learn what it takes to please an employer and become an asset to your workplace. By becoming a valued member of a team, you are setting yourself up for pay increases, additional training opportunities, and maybe even a path for future, more advanced, work.

Paying taxes and supporting community organizations with volunteer work and funds helps all of society. Your contributions make you a source of good for your state and country—and it all starts with your first job.

CHAPTER ONE

Preparing
for Work

Jobs have a number of requirements that employees will have to meet in order to be hired. First, workers need to follow the law by being at least the minimum age and having the correct citizenship status. Depending on the type of job, employees may need to drive, which requires a driver's license. Some jobs that require driving may provide workers with a vehicle; others require use of the employee's own vehicle. Certain positions require drug tests or vaccinations. Many employers insist that a worker have no criminal record. Almost all employers require references, or people who can vouch for the applicant's character and work ethic.

Legal Forms for Work

Every American worker (and citizens who do not work, too) should have a Social Security number and a Social Security card. Many children have Social Security cards and do not realize it.

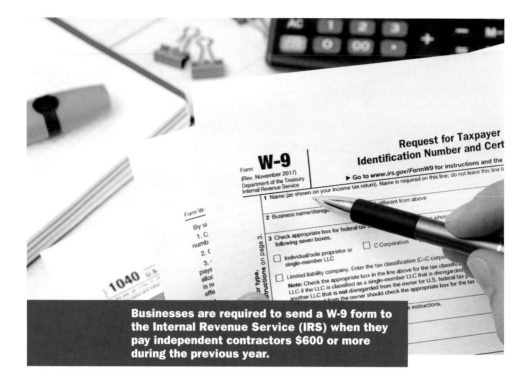

Businesses are required to send a W-9 form to the Internal Revenue Service (IRS) when they pay independent contractors $600 or more during the previous year.

When they were born, their parents may have applied for their Social Security number at the hospital, at the same time that they applied for a birth certificate. If so, the parents probably are keeping the child's card in a safe place. The child should not sign and use the card until 1) he or she reaches the age of eighteen or 2) begins work, if that occurs at an earlier age.

People who have never been issued a Social Security card can apply for it by visiting the nearest Social Security office or online. They must provide proof of identity and proof of US citizenship.

Citizens are advised not to carry their Social Security cards on their person. Rather, they should store them in secure places. If a purse or wallet is stolen and it contains the victim's Social Security card, the theft of that very private information can cause big problems.

Social Security is the system by which workers pay money into a government program throughout their working lives. The amount they pay in determines the amount they can receive back later. When they retire, or if they become disabled before retirement, their investment in the Social Security program can bring them regular government payments to provide income in difficult times.

Some states (not the federal government) require workers under the age of eighteen to obtain employment certificates and age certificates. These are called work papers. School guidance counselors can tell you whether or not these are required. They can probably furnish the forms you need to fill out or tell you how to obtain forms from the state government. Work papers typically require you to obtain a basic physical fitness checkup by a doctor and provide proof of age (birth certificate, driver's license, etc.). A parent or guardian's assistance may be required.

Contacting and Meeting Employers

You, a new job seeker, should begin by preparing a résumé. This document tells employers basic information about you, with an emphasis on special skills, previous experience, and personal interests. The résumé is an essential tool that you will update regularly and keep handy until retirement. The longer a person works, gains new experience, and obtains advanced education, the longer and more impressive the résumé will become.

There are different types of résumés. If you are a person with no work experience, you should develop what's called a functional résumé. Since you do not have previous jobs to describe, this résumé focuses on your skills and interests.

Once you have on-the-job experience, a chronological résumé may be more effective. This type presents your employment

Businesses usually require a résumé when you apply for a job. This document provides employers with more information about you than an application form can.

history job by job, beginning with the most recent. It can show how you are progressing in a particular career or area of experience.

Your name, address, phone number, and email address appear at the top of the résumé. Usually, the body of the résumé begins with a brief statement of objectives. Your overall objective in finding a job might be to serve a certain segment of the buying public. It may be to help people with special needs. It may be to protect the environment or improve the community. It may be to advance in the restaurant or hotel industries, drive a truck for a major distributing company, or sell houses. It may be to make furniture or clothes, write for a newspaper, or work with animals.

The résumé will then list your skills, any previous experience, and your education. It should let the employer know why you are a good candidate for a specific job. At the end, you should provide the names and contact information of at least three references. These are people who can recommend you for a job. Make sure you talk to these people and get their permission before naming them as references.

For most jobs, you will need to apply online. But if you apply for a job in person, you should bring a copy of your résumé for the employer to review and place on file. When applying by letter or email, you should enclose your résumé and a brief cover letter. A cover letter should have a catchy first sentence that gets the employer's attention. Busy employers may not spend more than a few seconds scanning a cover letter unless they immediately read something about the applicant that attracts them. For example,

An in-person job interview provides both employers and potential employees with the chance to get to know one another.

the letter should never begin, "I would like to apply for your advertised job as a sales assistant." The employer may read no further. A much more effective opening would be "I am eager to join your team as a sales assistant and help your business grow."

Most employers have applications for aspiring workers to fill out before an interview. Some applications lead to nothing; they are filed away, perhaps unread, and are eventually destroyed. If the employer is impressed by the application, the cover letter, and the résumé, the applicant will be called in for an interview when an appropriate job opening arises. First impressions are extremely important. You should dress neatly, arrive on time, and smile. The job seeker should be able to answer questions such as the following:

"Why do you want to work here?"
"What skills or interests do you possess that make you a good fit for this position?"
"What experiences have you had that show your strengths?"
"What would you like to be doing in five years?"

Being an Entrepreneur

Most teenagers are excited to go to work for an established business. A few are especially adventurous. Even while they're in school, they decide to start their own businesses and be their own bosses.

In most cases, student businesses are solo services. A teenager may be a good musician and become an instructor, setting up a schedule of private lessons—usually taught at the instructor's home. For some, babysitting or after-school child care (being a nanny) is a steady service. Computer whizzes can become after-school and weekend consultants, performing certain

Job Hunting Tips for Teens

Start writing your résumé. Even if you have little or no work experience and your résumé contains nothing more than your personal interests and contact information, it's the launching pad for your first job and your future career. Include even small jobs—pet sitting, yard maintenance, babysitting—in your first résumé.

Commit yourself to finishing high school. In most career fields, a higher education will lead to higher and faster advancement. At the least, you will need a high school diploma to find a wide choice of interesting job opportunities.

Let employed friends know you are interested in a part-time job while you're a student. They can tell you of openings where they work and point you to the hiring official. They also can explain what they like and dislike about their jobs.

Learn all you can about a job before you apply. If it isn't something you can or want to do, it will be difficult to find that out after you're hired.

Don't be late for a job interview, even by a minute.

Let the job interviewer know you're eager to join the team. Be able to explain why you prefer to work there—and nowhere else.

Don't be discouraged if, after an interview, you don't get a job offer. If you've made a good impression, the interviewer may call you when another opening comes up later.

computer tasks and solving technical problems for local businesses and individuals. Photography buffs may land freelance assignments from newspapers and magazines. The founder of such a service might have a partner who shares expenses, income, and tasks, but rarely hires employees.

Some services involve little or no overhead or out-of-pocket expenses. Others require basic tools (a computer, software, and attachments, perhaps). They may require travel (gasoline and auto maintenance are significant expenses). Advertising might be necessary, at least in the beginning.

Photography can provide you with income if you find the right places to sell your work.

In all businesses, the owner must have an effective system for collecting money, must keep accurate records, and must obey tax requirements. The more successful and complex the business, the more likely the worker will need a tax professional to make sure the operation follows all laws and regulations. A financial adviser also can explain which expenses are tax deductible.

CHAPTER TWO

The All-Important Dollar

Young people do not usually become rich from their first job. In fact, teens are among the lowest-paid members of the workforce. Jobs that teens qualify for usually require little prior experience and a basic education. Because so many people meet the requirements for experience and education, these jobs pay little. Still, first jobs provide many skills and benefits to workers.

The Law and Minimum Wage

The minimum wage is the least amount that employers are required to pay their workers. The US Department of Labor enforces the national minimum wage. At the time that the Fair Minimum Wage Act of 2007 became federal law, the federal minimum wage was $5.15 per hour. This law called for increases each July 24 for the following three years. The minimum wage

EMPLOYEE RIGHTS
UNDER THE FAIR LABOR STANDARDS ACT

FEDERAL MINIMUM WAGE
$7.25 PER HOUR
BEGINNING JULY 24, 2009

The law requires employers to display this poster where employees can readily see it.

OVERTIME PAY
At least 1½ times the regular rate of pay for all hours worked over 40 in a workweek.

CHILD LABOR
An employee must be at least 16 years old to work in most non-farm jobs and at least 18 to work in non-farm jobs declared hazardous by the Secretary of Labor. Youths 14 and 15 years old may work outside school hours in various non-manufacturing, non-mining, non-hazardous jobs with certain work hours restrictions. Different rules apply in agricultural employment.

TIP CREDIT
Employers of "tipped employees" who meet certain conditions may claim a partial wage credit based on tips received by their employees. Employers must pay tipped employees a cash wage of at least $2.13 per hour if they claim a tip credit against their minimum wage obligation. If an employee's tips combined with the employer's cash wage of at least $2.13 per hour do not equal the minimum hourly wage, the employer must make up the difference.

NURSING MOTHERS
The FLSA requires employers to provide reasonable break time for a nursing mother employee who is subject to the FLSA's overtime requirements in order for the employee to express breast milk for her nursing child for one year after the child's birth each time such employee has a need to express breast milk. Employers are also required to provide a place, other than a bathroom, that is shielded from view and free from intrusion from coworkers and the public, which may be used by the employee to express breast milk.

ENFORCEMENT
The Department has authority to recover back wages and an equal amount in liquidated damages in instances of minimum wage, overtime, and other violations. The Department may litigate and/or recommend criminal prosecution. Employers may be assessed civil money penalties for each willful or repeated violation of the minimum wage or overtime pay provisions of the law. Civil money penalties may also be assessed for violations of the FLSA's child labor provisions. Heightened civil money penalties may be assessed for each child labor violation that results in the death or serious injury of any minor employee, and such assessments may be doubled when the violations are determined to be willful or repeated. The law also prohibits retaliating against or discharging workers who file a complaint or participate in any proceeding under the FLSA.

ADDITIONAL INFORMATION
- Certain occupations and establishments are exempt from the minimum wage, and/or overtime pay provisions.
- Special provisions apply to workers in American Samoa, the Commonwealth of the Northern Mariana Islands, and the Commonwealth of Puerto Rico.
- Some state laws provide greater employee protections; employers must comply with both.
- Some employers incorrectly classify workers as "independent contractors" when they are actually employees under the FLSA. It is important to know the difference between the two because employees (unless exempt) are entitled to the FLSA's minimum wage and overtime pay protections and correctly classified independent contractors are not.
- Certain full-time students, student learners, apprentices, and workers with disabilities may be paid less than the minimum wage under special certificates issued by the Department of Labor.

WHD WAGE AND HOUR DIVISION
UNITED STATES DEPARTMENT OF LABOR

1-866-487-9243
TTY: 1-877-889-5627
www.dol.gov/whd

WH1088 REV 07/16

The Fair Labor Standards Act (FLSA) Minimum Wage Poster must be posted in a conspicuous spot in all places of employment.

increased to $5.85 per hour in July 2007, to $6.55 per hour in July 2008, and to $7.25 per hour in July 2009.

Under the US Department of Labor's Youth Minimum Wage Program, workers under age twenty can be paid substantially less than the federal minimum wage during the first ninety calendar days (in other words, not just workdays) of employment. Their minimum wage during the trial period is $4.25 per hour. After three months (or beginning on their twentieth birthday, whichever occurs first), they must be paid the standard minimum wage.

Many states have their own minimum wage laws. About half the states have set minimum wage levels higher than that of the federal government. Seven states either have lower minimum wages than the national requirement or set no minimum wage at all.

Farmworkers and other agricultural workers are not covered by mandatory minimum wage laws.

In states that have minimum wages different from that of the US government, the higher wage is enforced.

Not every worker qualifies to receive the minimum wage. Many agricultural jobs are not covered. The law does not cover certain individuals who have disabilities that prevent them from being fully productive.

A special law applies to full-time students. Their employers are required to pay only 85 percent of the minimum wage. Also under special terms are "student-learners." These are high school students who are taking vocational courses. Employers in their areas of training can hire them at a lower wage (75 percent of the minimum wage). In return, the employers provide them, while still in high school, with on-the-job experience that will help them get jobs when they graduate.

Varying Pay Scales

Some jobs involve odd pay structures that can change an employee's income greatly from day to day and month to month. People in sales, for example, usually work on commission. They are paid a percentage of the amount they sell. Commission percentages vary, and sales trends go up and down. Sometimes, the salesperson can sell a product very quickly. Then, it may be days or weeks before another sale is made.

Suppose a seller of furniture is working on a commission of 10 percent. One day, the salesperson sells $1,000 worth of furniture. Ten percent of $1,000 is $100. If the person works approximately eight hours per day, the earnings on that day would be $12.50 per hour ($100 divided by eight hours). The next day, the person sells only $100 worth of furniture, receiving a commission of $10 (10 percent of $100). That means the person earns only $1.25 per hour on that day ($10 divided by eight hours).

Because sales patterns can be unpredictable, many companies pay their sales staff a salary plus commission. Depending on the business, the salary might be as low as the minimum wage. On the other hand, some companies pay very well to keep good salespeople happy during downturns in sales.

Some salespeople earn hundreds of thousands of dollars each year. Others don't earn enough to survive. Young people interested in sales jobs should be aware of the risks. They should think twice before taking a sales job that pays only a commission. They should also be wary of unknown companies that promise unbelievably high earnings.

Another class of wage earner with a special pay scale is the tipped employee, most notably waitstaff. Federal law requires the

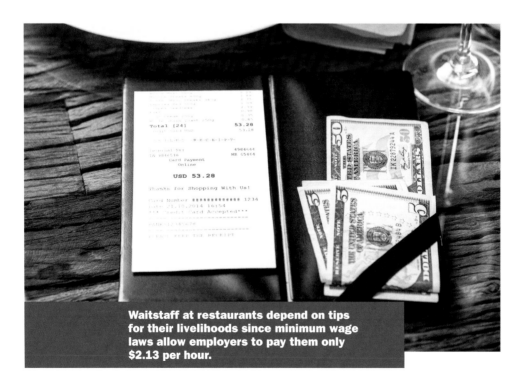

Waitstaff at restaurants depend on tips for their livelihoods since minimum wage laws allow employers to pay them only $2.13 per hour.

employer to pay only $2.13 per hour, apart from tips—assuming certain conditions are met. The law requires that this base pay plus tips must add up to at least the minimum wage. If it doesn't, the employer must increase the base pay. A number of states have laws requiring a higher base pay for tipped workers.

Tipped employees in some situations do well. Some of them earn many times more money in tips than they draw in base pay.

Beyond Salary

A good job gives employees good benefits. Many smart job searchers are as interested in the benefits as they are in the pay.

A typical benefit is health insurance. Group (company) health insurance benefits vary widely. Some policies cover almost everything for their employees, including long-term hospitalization, regular medical checkups, and full dental and vision care. Other policies cover only medical emergencies. Health policies also differ in the amount of deductible that the worker must pay. For example, the employee may have to pay the first $200, $500, or $1,000 of any medical expense; the insurance company will pay the rest. Sometimes that means the employee must pay the total cost. If an emergency room visit costs $800 and the policy's deductible is $500, the injured employee must pay $500 and the insurer pays only the remaining $300. But long-term hospitalizations can easily cost $50,000, well worth the $500 deductible.

Some companies also provide life insurance. These policies might pay a year's salary—or several years' salary—to the spouse or family if the employee dies.

Many employers pay or help pay for employee retirement plans like 401(k)s. In 401(k) accounts, the employee's taxes are put off until withdrawal, and he or she usually chooses the types

Jobs often offer employees paid vacation time to spend however they like, whether at home or other places, such as the beach.

of investments that are in the account. Some employers pay into investment programs.

Paid vacation and personal leave/sick time (in addition to holidays) are other benefits. In most workplaces, employees get increasing amounts of annual leave the longer they stay with the company. Some employers offer family leave (time off from work for a parent who has just had a child) at full pay. Some provide free family, financial, and legal counseling to employees who need it.

Myths and Facts

Myth High school and college students don't have to pay taxes.

Fact They do have to pay taxes if they earn above a certain amount of money in a year. They need to know the tax requirements of both their state and federal governments.

Myth Teenagers are paid at least the minimum wage.

Fact Many of them are. But by federal law, for their first ninety days on the job, they can be paid substantially less. Full-time students and student-learners may also receive less than the minimum wage.

Myth It's better to find a job as waitstaff than as a cashier or restaurant host/hostess. Waitstaff don't have to pay taxes on the tips they make.

Fact It may be a better job simply because tipped employees often enjoy remarkably high incomes. However, they have to pay taxes on all of their earnings. They report their tips to their employer, who in turn reports the annual total to state and federal tax agencies. A server who is hiding tips is breaking the law.

CHAPTER **THREE**

Work on a Schedule

The first thing that most people do when they find a job is to calculate how much it pays. There are only two factors in this simple formula: hourly wage and number of hours. You, as a teen, won't find a very wide range in hourly wages. For most student jobs, roughly minimum wage, give or take a dollar an hour, is what you can expect to be paid. The number of hours worked, then, is the main factor in determining how much you will earn.

Before committing to any job, you must carefully weigh work time against other responsibilities. Time for schoolwork is most important. So is time for after-school clubs or sports. Time for household chores must be considered. A certain amount of downtime—time for recreation, friends, and family—is necessary each week. And, of course, you have to sleep sometime. In the end, you must decide which pursuits are most important during the teen years. How much time are you willing to devote to work?

While you do not need advanced math skills to calculate how much money you will be earning from your new job, you will probably want to figure out how much to expect from your paychecks.

Labor Laws and Teens

When a teenager becomes eighteen, there are no employment age requirements under law. (Some types of jobs require that a worker be at least twenty-one to hold the job.) Until then, students may be limited in the number of hours they can work and in the kinds of jobs they can hold. Besides laws that are enforced by the US Department of Labor, some states enforce special child labor laws. Because labor laws change and vary from state to state, teenagers should ask their school guidance counselors about their employment options.

Jobs with the potential to be unsafe, such as those that involve using tools like power saws, are not available to employees seventeen and younger.

Employees ages sixteen and seventeen can work any number of hours, except in jobs that the Department of Labor considers unsafe. (Power saws, mixing and grinding devices, and other types of equipment can make a workplace unsafe under child labor laws.) You might qualify for a payroll job at age fourteen or fifteen, but work hours will be limited: no more than three hours per day, eighteen hours per week during the school term (full-time work is allowed in the summer). Most fourteen- and fifteen-year-olds are not allowed to work later than 7:00 p.m. when school is in session or later than 9:00 p.m. in the summer. Teenagers who work under terms of the Department of Labor's full-time student program can work no more than eight hours a day, twenty hours a week, during

Many teenagers find their first jobs as cashiers in fast-food restaurants or many other types of businesses.

the school term. They can work forty-hour weeks during summer and winter breaks.

There are exceptions to the general rules. For instance, in most cases, children younger than fourteen are allowed to work in shops, stores, and restaurants owned by their parents. Child entertainers (in radio, TV, movies, or stage presentations) are not subject to Fair Labor Standards Act time limitations.

Organizing Your Time

Regardless of the laws, you should think about your time very carefully before entering the workforce. Going to work is a life

Temporary Jobs

Some students, after carefully considering how they want to spend their time, decide to limit their employment to summer and seasonal jobs. Many employers hire more teenagers during the summer, when they might need more help. Holiday periods also present good opportunities for young workers, especially in retail stores when they need extra help to keep up with the mad holiday rush.

If they learn to save their seasonal earnings and manage their money wisely, teenagers can stretch their short-term incomes to meet their spending needs throughout the year. Holiday work doesn't interfere with their studies. And when school is out of session, they can work full-time hours.

change. A job that involves weeknight work obviously interferes with regular homework time. Can you find time to complete assignments (before going to work after school, late at night, early in the morning before classes begin)? Will this be too stressful?

It will be helpful to find a first job that offers an adaptable work schedule. Otherwise, you will have to arrange the rest of your life around the job.

Above all, the first job will force you to learn a new kind of discipline. Frequently arriving late for work will likely cause you to lose the job. So will slack performance. A bad attitude about

When you have a job, be sure to set aside time to complete your homework so you don't find yourself burning the midnight oil.

the work, unfriendliness toward other employees, and constant clock-watching are unlikely to lead to promotions. Getting fired from a job definitely will not look good on a résumé. If you are unhappy, the best remedy is to continue performing as well as possible while seeking a new job. If a new job cannot be found, resign while you are still on good terms with the management. In the long run, it's best for you to bow out of the situation gracefully than to be dismissed for poor performance.

CHAPTER **FOUR**

Strategies for Spending

A lthough it can be tempting to spend all the money you earn, that is a bad idea. Learning how to budget now will save you a lot of future headaches. A simple budget shows income and expenses from week to week, month to month, or paycheck to paycheck. Income is how much money a person receives. The expense part of the budget worksheet shows each purchase. A good budget should be able to tell you exactly how every dollar is spent. A solid understanding of that is necessary to avoid financial trouble.

Where It All Goes

Until you begin a job and create a budget, personal finances— the income and outgo of money—are vague. The budget is like a bright light that illuminates the good and the bad things about income and expenses. A budget is a changing picture. It

Budgets can be complex, like this one, or simple. The important thing is that they account for your income and expenses.

is regularly adjusted with new information. Every time money is received or spent, it changes the budget.

Many people examine their budget reports at the end of every month. Some revise their budgets each week. The most devoted budget keepers look at their worksheets every day. For others, it makes the most sense to review the budget at the end of each pay period.

Whatever budget period you want to use, the objective is to balance the budget. In a balanced budget, expenses never exceed income. If spending is more than income during any given budget period, the situation must be corrected quickly. If it isn't, a short-term budget problem can grow into a financial crisis that might take years to untangle.

An example of a balanced monthly budget is as follows:

October 2020

Income

Marko Theater Company	$	211.25
Total income	$	211.25

Expenses

ice cream	$	3.00
music downloads	$	20.00
birthday gift for Dana	$	21.00
clothes	$	58.00
lunch with friends	$	6.00
gas	$	40.00
cosmetics	$	15.00
dinner with friends	$	12.00
Total expenses	$	175.00
Cash on hand		
($211.25 − 175.00 = $36.25)	$	36.25

The following is an example of an unbalanced monthly budget:

November 2020

Income

Marko Theater Company	$	196.14
Total income	$	196.14

Expenses

movie	$	7.50
DVD purchase	$	20.00
music downloads	$	9.00
dinner with friends	$	10.00
bargain DVD purchase	$	6.00

T-shirt	$	13.50
shoes	$	45.00
two pairs of jeans	$	70.00
lunch with friends	$	7.00
gas	$	38.00
cosmetics	$	15.00
dinner with friends	$	12.00
Total expenses	$	253.00
Overspending amount		
($196.14 - $253.00 = -$56.86) -$		56.86

Notice that every expense should be entered separately into the budget worksheet. Do not fail to enter minor expenses. It's a good idea to record the dates of income checks and expenses.

If you are spending more than earning, the situation must be reversed. Solutions: spend less or earn more. A simple budget reveals why few people can buy everything they want.

Every sound budget will have an additional line item not shown in these examples: savings deposit. Beginning with your first job, you should commit to saving a specific amount from each paycheck. During budget periods when the numbers look particularly bright, more money can go into savings.

A budget is also a valuable planning tool. A person who wants to make a special purchase can determine in advance if (and when) it is affordable. This is done by calculating expected income and expenses for the next budget period and comparing them with recent budget reports. The results will probably present various possibilities, such as the following:

- "Should be no problem. I can buy it right now."
- "If I work four extra hours this month and keep my expenses at the same level as last month, I can afford it."

• "If I don't eat out or buy any clothes this month, I can afford it."

• "There's no way I can afford this right now without getting into serious money trouble."

Depositing and Withdrawing

When they receive their paychecks, workers take them to their banks and deposit them into their checking accounts or use a smartphone app to make a mobile deposit. Many employees have their employers deposit their earnings directly into their bank accounts via electronic transfers instead of receiving a physical check or cash. Workers might do several other things with the money from the paycheck at that time. They may take out a small amount of cash for their wallets. Those who are wise deposit a portion of their earnings into savings accounts. If they can afford to, they can put some of their income into investments.

Young people cannot open checking accounts until they are eighteen years old, unless an adult cosigns the account. That means the adult agrees to be responsible for the account if the teenager spends recklessly. For example, if the young customer has $500 in the checking account and writes checks amounting to $600 without depositing more money, the account is overdrawn by $100. After an account becomes overdrawn, the bank will refuse to honor the checks that are written. It will "bounce" them back to the businesses or individuals to whom they were paid. It's costly to overdraw a checking account and bounce checks. The account holder must deposit funds into the checking account before it can be used again. Worse, the customer will probably have to pay an overdraft fee to the bank, plus a returned-check fee to the victim of the bounce. The incident can stain the person's

If you have a smartphone, mobile deposits can save you a trip to the bank or an ATM when you need to deposit a check.

credit record. A history of check bouncing can hurt the individual's future attempts to obtain credit and get a job.

On the other hand, a teenager can open a savings account at a younger age. There is no danger of overdrafts with a savings account because there is no check writing. The customer must go to the bank to withdraw money or request the bank by phone or online to move funds from the savings account to a different account. The bank will not transfer more money from savings than the customer has available in the account.

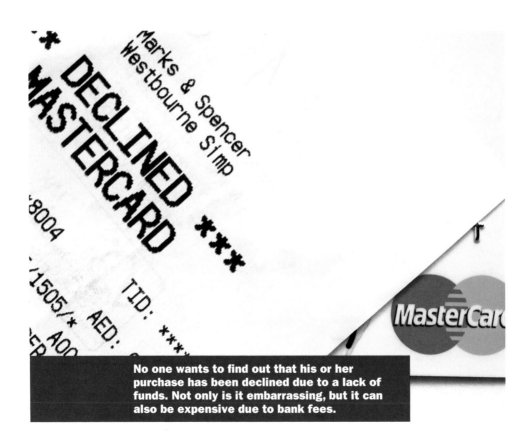

No one wants to find out that his or her purchase has been declined due to a lack of funds. Not only is it embarrassing, but it can also be expensive due to bank fees.

Good Habits and Long-Term Benefits

Some working teenagers have only savings accounts. Each time they receive a paycheck, they keep some of the money in cash for spending but deposit most of it into savings. Unless they really need to pay for things frequently by debit card or check, it's a smart way to handle the income from their first job. It's exciting to watch a savings account grow. What makes it even more exciting is something called interest.

Visit your bank in person to set up investment accounts. Bankers can help you with questions and recommendations.

When customers deposit money into savings accounts for long periods of time, the bank uses the money to make loans to other people. When those people pay back the borrowed money, they must pay the bank an additional fee—the interest on the loan. The bank, in turn, pays a small percentage of interest to its customers who have savings accounts. It does not pay its savers nearly as much in interest as it charges its borrowers. (That is how the bank makes money.) For example, it may charge an interest rate of 5 or 10 percent (or higher) on a loan. It may pay less than 1 percent interest to savings account holders. But the interest for the saver adds up. And since interest earned is a percentage of the money that you have in the bank, the more money you deposit, the more interest you can earn.

There is a way to earn even more interest with savings. Money can be invested in a special, long-term account. In an investment account, the bank customer agrees to leave money in a special bank account for a year, five years, ten years, or longer. The customer cannot withdraw the money during the investment period without being charged an early-withdrawal fee. However, in the end, the investment can earn the customer several times more interest than a regular savings account. For young employees who are saving much of their incomes and who know they won't need the money for a while, investing is wise money management.

Many forms of investment are available. Banks can set up money market accounts based on international stock markets. Some employers encourage their workers to invest by establishing individual retirement accounts (IRAs) and 401(k) plans. Many workers buy stocks or bonds. Having a financial adviser is strongly recommended to sort out the options for employees who are interested in long-term investing.

Note that most investments require that the customer deposit a large amount of money for a long period of time. That makes it difficult for many teenage employees to become investors. The typical way to break into investing is to start a standard savings account. When the account balance exceeds

Keeping Your Identity

Identity theft has alarmed workers and consumers in recent years. Stalkers have been known to swipe personal identification information from citizens' street garbage. Far more clever stalkers use the internet, looking for weaknesses in web browsers and email systems that let them into the personal computers and private lives of unsuspecting individuals.

Some internet observers claim it is at least as safe—possibly safer—to do business online as on paper. Others believe the internet has opened a can of worms when it comes to financial security.

You may not see them, but hackers are constantly at work to find ways to steal your hard-earned money.

(continued on the next page)

(continued from the previous page)

Hackers, they warn, can obtain every detail from worms when it comes to financial security, everything from the user's Social Security number to banking and credit card account numbers.

Every expert agrees that a computer security program is needed if a worker plans to bank online. That includes security of the user's web browser. But will software security be enough? The question lingers.

$1,000, consider converting some or all of the savings to a long-term investment.

Money in Cyberspace

Many people believe that all finances are going electronic and online. For years, shoppers have been ordering products online. They have paid with their credit or debit cards. The payment goes into the seller's bank account. Neither the buyer nor the seller ever touches real money.

Increasingly, many people now prefer to pay their bills over the internet. It is very fast and easy. It is also automated. That means the same payment process is repeated each month. The customer enters the new monthly payment numbers, clicks once or twice with the computer mouse, and the computer system does the rest. The customer might allow a phone company, utility company, or insurance company to withdraw monthly payments automatically from his or her checking account. The customer never has to write and mail a check.

Online bill paying saves you the time of writing out checks and the expense of mailing them or visiting the organizations in person.

Similarly, an advantage of having paychecks directly deposited is fast processing. Workers who receive paychecks in person on the fifteenth of the month might not be able to deposit them until the sixteenth or later. A direct, electronic deposit can be credited to the account on the fifteenth—perhaps even earlier.

Some say the internet has made paper and metal money objects of the past. Do people really need coins and bills? Almost every purchase and payment can be made with a plastic credit or debit card or processed automatically by employers and banks.

CHAPTER FIVE

Responsibilities to the Government and Society

There are two things certain in life: death and taxes. Even teenagers with part-time, seasonal work must often pay taxes to the government. The Internal Revenue Service (IRS), a branch of the US Department of the Treasury, handles taxes owed to the federal government. Workers are also responsible for taxes to the states they live in.

A worker who is self-employed must keep track of how much of the earnings should go to state and federal governments. The individual makes estimated tax payments to state and federal tax agencies each quarter. At the end of the year, the person (or a tax professional) calculates the total income, deductible expenses, and taxes that were due. If the individual has paid more in quarterly estimates than was necessary, a tax refund should result. If the self-employed worker underpaid in quarterly estimates, he or she must pay the remainder by April 15.

Most workers are employed by businesses. The employer withholds a share of state and federal taxes from each paycheck. The amount withheld (which the employer pays to the government on behalf of the employee) is based on tax formulas for the current year. At the end of the year, the employee (or a tax professional) must calculate total earnings, taxes paid, and possible deductions. It may be that the worker can deduct certain job-related expenses. In that case, the employee should receive a tax refund.

The IRS employed nearly seventy-seven thousand people in 2017. That same year, their operating budget topped $11.5 billion.

Paycheck Deductions

Most paychecks include a stub, which is an attached form that the employee keeps as a record. It shows details about how the pay was processed. You should notice first the "gross pay" and "net pay" entries. Gross pay is the total amount the employer pays. If you have clocked ten hours during the pay period and are being paid $10 an hour, the gross pay will be $100 (ten hours times $10).

However, the paycheck probably will be for a lower amount— the net pay. The employer takes out federal and state taxes (including state unemployment and state disability insurance), Social Security,

Where Taxes Go

Employees' tax dollars pay for a wide variety of public services. Part of the money pays for national defense. Part of it pays for social services—to help support Americans who can't find work, are unable to work, or need other types of assistance. Taxes pay for law enforcement and prison facilities, keeps roads in good condition, widens some of them because of increasing traffic, and builds new ones. Tax money pays for public education and government research in science and other areas. These funds pay government office holders' salaries and benefits. Many other public programs and services are also funded by workers' taxes.

The salaries of state and local public servants are just some of the expenses funded by your taxes.

Social Security is what the federal government describes as "a system of social insurance." A small portion of an employee's earnings goes into the system; the employer must pay a matching amount. The Social Security Administration uses this money to pay benefits to older workers who have retired. Eventually, when today's young worker reaches retirement age, the paycheck deductions of future workers will pay the current worker's own retirement benefits. Retirees are not the only beneficiaries of Social Security. Children whose parents are retired, disabled, or deceased might receive Social Security money. Injured workers can receive disability pay.

Medicare is a similar federal program. It helps pay for the medical needs of people who are ages sixty-five and older, especially for hospital stays, doctor bills, medicine, and related expenses.

Medicare, and possibly other deductions. (For instance, employees are responsible for paying a portion of the company insurance plan if they are insured on that plan.) After subtracting all these deductions, the net pay—the amount of the check—results. This is commonly known as the take-home pay. The pay stub will usually indicate not just what the deductions are for the current pay period but the amount of deductions for the whole year, up to that point. The label "YTD" in any section of the pay stub means "year to date"—the amount of earnings or deductions since the beginning of the year.

The pay stub shows the beginning and ending dates of the pay period, the employee's name, tax status (dependent, single, married, etc.), and probably an employee number. Some employers provide very detailed pay stubs. They might keep track of vacation and sick leave, for example. If the employee has the money directly deposited into a personal checking or savings account, that information (including the account number) will be shown.

Requirements and Rules

Not all teenagers are subject to identical tax requirements. In most families, a parent can claim one or more children as dependents. This means the parents can claim a special tax deduction on their own earnings because of the usual costs of supporting a dependent child. A dependent child who gets a job may or may not have to file a separate tax return each year. It depends largely on the amount of the child's earned income (wages, salary, or—if self-employed—fees received). Unearned income, such as savings account interest, is also a factor.

The IRS (www.irs.gov) provides details about federal tax requirements on its website. For information about a state's requirements, you should find the website of the state's department of revenue or taxes. A school guidance counselor can provide basic information about tax requirements for you. Tax professionals and financial advisers can also provide detailed information about your specific situation.

Even when the federal law exempts a teenager from filing a tax return, the IRS advises that you file a return in certain situations. For example, if you had income tax withheld from paychecks, you might qualify for a tax refund.

By becoming familiar with your pay stub, you will have a good grasp of your income and paycheck withdrawals.

Helping Others

Earning money is a good feeling. Giving some of it to worthy causes is an even nicer feeling. At an early age, you should consider giving a portion of the paycheck back to society.

Needy organizations and individuals are everywhere. You may choose to give a tithe (a tenth) to a church. The Red Cross

Volunteers for Habitat for Humanity work together to build homes for needy families.

and other relief organizations constantly need funds. Nonprofit agencies seek contributions to protect the environment, feed hungry people in third world countries (and in poverty-stricken areas of the United States), and raise money for people with special needs. They also preserve historic landmarks and support the arts.

There are countless community causes, too. For example, a high school band may be raising funds for an appearance in the Thanksgiving Day parade in New York City or for new instruments. A neighborhood organization may want street beautification. Or a civic club will sponsor a trip to Disney World for area children with muscular dystrophy if it can raise enough money.

Some contributions are tax deductible. When it comes time to file annual tax returns, the giver can subtract those contributions from the income that is reported to the government and pay less in taxes. To some contributors, it does not matter whether the donation is deductible or not; the cause is what's important. Still, it makes sense to find out if any contribution can result in savings at April tax time.

CHAPTER SIX

Jobs and Your Future

Graduation marks the accomplishment of an educational goal. Enjoy that good feeling—you earned it!

No matter how long you work, you will remember your first job. That job can be a stepping-stone to better employment in the future and a source of pride in your accomplishments when you recall the past.

At least as important are the life skills—especially financial skills—the first job will bring. You will either learn to become a smart income manager or squander much of the hard-earned money and look back in disappointment in later years.

Even though your first job may not be what you want to do for a living, it can be a first step toward a career. By high school graduation, many students have a vague idea where they want to go with their vocations. By college graduation, most students have a much clearer plan. They are actively exploring the job market and already may have obtained related work experience.

Attitude Matters

"Whistle While You Work" is the title of a classic song from the *Snow White and the Seven Dwarfs* animated movie. It has to do with a person's attitude. If possible, you should look for a first job that will be enjoyable. All jobs require workers to perform boring or difficult tasks sometimes. Unless it is truly necessary, though, you should resist pursuing a job opportunity simply for the purpose of making money. You should seek a first job in which you look forward to going to work. At the same time, a job should begin teaching you about the business

Jobs don't have to be miserable—strive to find ones that you enjoy.

side of life and, if possible, provide experience toward your future career path.

Even if it pays well, a bad first job can have negative financial effects in the long run. It can dampen your desire to stand out and advance. It can create an early impression that a job is something to be endured, not enjoyed. The result can be a lifelong cycle of unsatisfying employment. If you are not motivated to do your best, your prospects for promotions and other job opportunities are poor. So try to find a job that you will enjoy doing.

Looking for a Better Job

If you find a good job, you will want to keep it. You will work hard and demonstrate honesty, reliability, and a cheerful attitude. Meanwhile, you will be acquiring life skills that can be obtained only in the workplace. These include time management and money management. During the months or years of employment, you can be building a nice savings account and may even be making long-term investments.

A first job is almost never the last. The time

Good performance at a first job is an important step toward your future employment goals.

will come for you to move on—maybe before high school graduation. Ideally, when it's time to take a better job, you will leave on good terms with the first employer. The first employer can be an important reference for many years to come. However, as time passes, the employer might close the business or move away. It's a good idea for you to obtain a letter of reference from the first boss. The letter should be dated and addressed "To Whom It May Concern," and it will hopefully contain a glowing recommendation to any future employer.

A first job is the beginning of an individual's working life. It could lead to a career; it might not. A sixteen-year-old who lands a job as a supermarket checkout clerk might go on to become a psychologist. A seventeen-year-old who runs errands for a law firm might go on to become a supermarket manager. On the other hand, a teenager who works after school as a veterinarian's assistant just might go on to become a veterinarian.

Whatever the job, it's an important first step for you. You should learn as much from the experience as possible. Almost always, it will teach priceless lessons about money.

And there's one special thing about your first job: you never forget it.

Great Questions to Ask a Financial Adviser

1. Do I have to pay taxes on money I earn before I turn twenty-one? Before eighteen? Before fourteen?

2. Do I have to pay taxes on money I earn doing odd jobs like mowing lawns, babysitting, or teaching guitar or tennis?

3. If I become a salesperson and work totally on commission, will I have to pay taxes?

4. Am I limited in the number of hours I can work each week until I reach a certain age?

5. How old must I be before I can get a "real job," with a regular paycheck?

6. My cousin in another state works for the same fast-food restaurant chain I work for. We have the same job title, perform the same tasks, and receive the same hourly wage. A higher percentage of my earnings is withheld than hers. Why?

7. What can I do to make part of my income tax exempt?

8. How old must I be before I can start my own company or professional service?

9. What types of employee benefits should I expect in my first job?

10. Do I need an accountant or tax professional to make sure I don't get in trouble with the government?

GLOSSARY

benefits Job perks in addition to pay, including financial assistance in case of emergencies and retirement, paid vacation time, and other rewards.

bond A type of investment in which an individual helps the government or a corporation pay for a special project and earns interest in return.

budget A financial system that shows an individual, company, or organization how much money comes in and exactly how it is spent.

credit record The history and rating of how a person handles debts.

deductible An amount of a health or damage insurance claim that the insured person must pay before the insurance company begins its coverage; also, an expense that lowers taxable income.

deposit To put money into a bank account.

exempt Free of obligation; not required to obey certain laws or rules.

income Money a person receives in the form of paychecks, gifts, and sales.

interest A percentage of a borrowed amount of money that must be paid to the lender or investor, in addition to the original amount.

invest To put part of one's income into a financial plan with the purposes of increasing that amount.

IRA Individual retirement account; part of a worker's pay that is automatically deducted and invested in a special savings account.

money market account A savings account that usually pays higher interest than a regular savings account.

overdraft An amount of money written from a checking account that exceeds the balance available in the account.

overhead Ongoing business expenses, such as leasing office space and paying for water and electricity services.

salary Income earned from employment.

stock Part of the ownership of a company, also known as a share.

stock market A place where stocks are bought and sold by investors.

tax exemption A portion of earnings on which taxes do not have to be paid.

tax refund The government's year-end return to a citizen of tax money that was overpaid from payroll deductions during the year.

wage The amount a worker is paid by the hour.

FOR MORE INFORMATION

Canadian Legal Information Institute
World Exchange Plaza
1810 – 45 O'Connor Street
Ottawa, ON K1P 1A4
Canada
Website: http://www.canlii.org
> This institute provides information about Canadian labor laws. See especially the "Canada Labor Code" section (https://www.canlii.org/en/ca/laws/stat /rsc-1985-c-l-2/latest).

Human Resources and Social Development Canada
Labor Program
Human Resources and Social Development Canada
Ottawa, ON K1A 0J2
Canada
Website: https://www.canada.ca/en/employment-social -development/corporate/portfolio/labour.html
Twitter: @Labour_ESDC
Instagram: @esdc.edsc
This is Canada's federal labor department, which protects both workers' and employers' rights.

Internal Revenue Service (IRS)
US Department of the Treasury
1500 Pennsylvania Avenue NW
Washington, DC 20220

(202) 622-2000

Website: http://www.irs.gov

Facebook: @IRS

Twitter: @IRSnews

The IRS is the branch of the Treasury Department that
oversees taxes. Learn how much you owe at this
extensive site.

US Bureau of Labor Statistics (BLS)

2 Massachusetts Avenue NE

Washington, DC 20212-0001

(202) 691-5200

Website: http://www.bls.gov

Twitter: @BLS_gov

A labor fact-finding and economics agency within the US
Department of Labor, the BLS has a "Jobseeker or
Worker" resource section (http://www.bls.gov
/audience/jobseekers.htm).

US Department of Labor

Frances Perkins Building

200 Constitution Avenue NW

Washington, DC 20210

(866) 487-2365

Website: http://www.dol.gov

Facebook: @departmentoflabor

Twitter: @USDOL

This is the federal government agency that is responsible
for enforcing labor laws.

US Occupational Safety & Health Administration

200 Constitution Avenue NW

Washington, DC 20210
(800) 321-6742
Website: http://www.osha.gov
Facebook: @departmentoflabor
Twitter and Instagram: @usdol
This department provides job safety information. See
    especially the section for teenage employees
    (http://www.osha.gov/SLTC/teenworkers/index
    .html).

US Social Security Administration
Office of Public Inquiries
Windsor Park Building
6401 Security Boulevard
Baltimore, MD 21235
(800) 772-1213
Website: http://www.ssa.gov
Facebook and Twitter: @socialsecurity
This office is the federal agency that oversees the Social
    Security program, which requires a deduction from
    most workers' paychecks.

Youth Rules!
866-4USWAGE (1-866-487-9243)
Website: https://www.youthrules.gov
Run by the US Department of Labor, this site is geared
    toward young workers, providing answers to
    questions and concerns about their first jobs.

FOR FURTHER READING

Henneberg, Susan. *Step-by-Step Guide to Effective Job Hunting & Career Preparedness.* New York, NY: Rosen Publishing, 2015.

Higgins, M. G. *Finding and Keeping a Job.* Costa Mesa, CA: Saddleback Educational Publishing, 2017.

Hubbard, Rita. *Getting a Job in the Food Industry.* New York, NY: Rosen Publishing, 2017.

Jacobson, Ryan, and Jon Cannell. *Get a Summer Adventure Job.* Minneapolis, MN: Lerner Publications Company, 2015.

La Bella, Laura. *Getting a Job in the Retail Industry.* New York, NY: Rosen Publishing, 2017.

McGuire, Kara. *The Teen Money Manual: A Guide to Cash, Credit, Spending, Saving, Work, Wealth, and More.* North Mankato, MN: Capstone Young Readers, 2015.

Rauf, Don. *Getting Paid to Manage Social Media.* New York, NY: Rosen Publishing, 2017.

Sack, Rebekah. *The Young Adult's Survival Guide to Interviews: Finding the Job and Nailing the Interview.* Ocala, FL: Atlantic Publishing Group, Inc., 2016.

Uhl, Xina M., and Judy Monroe Peterson. *Making a Budget.* New York, NY: Rosen Publishing, 2020.

Uhl, Xina M., and Jeri Freedman. *Managing Bank Accounts and Investments.* New York, NY: Rosen Publishing, 2020.

BIBLIOGRAPHY

Brainerd, Jackson. "State Minimum Wages |
    2018 Minimum Wage by State." Affirmative Action |
    Overview. http://www.ncsl.org/research/labor-and
    -employment/state-minimum-wage-chart.aspx.

Bureau of Labor Statistics. *Occupational Outlook
    Handbook*. U.S. Department of Labor. Retrieved on
    October 18, 2018. https://www.bls.gov/ooh.

Doyle, Alison. "Child Labor Law." The Balance Careers.
    Retrieved on October 18, 2018. https://
    www.thebalancecareers.com/child-labor-laws-and
    -regulations-2060478.

Doyle, Alison. "How to Start Your First Job Search." The
    Balance Careers. Retrieved on October 18, 2018.
    https://www.thebalancecareers.com/how-to-find
    -your-first-job-2063898.

Doyle, Alison. "What Is the Best Way to Apply for a Part-
    Time Position?" The Balance Careers. Retrieved on
    October 18, 2018. http://jobsearch.about.com/od
    /parttimejobs/a/applyparttime.htm.

Doyle, Alison. "Tips for Finding a Job for Teens." The
    Balance Careers. Retrieved on October 18, 2018.
    https://www.thebalancecareers.com/tips-for-finding
    -a-job-for-teens-2058651.

Internal Revenue Service. *Publication 501: Exemptions,
    Standard Deduction and Filing Information*.
    Retrieved on October 18, 2018. https://www.irs
    .gov/publications/p501#d0e955.

JIST Editors. *Exploring Careers: A Young Person's Guide to 1,000 Jobs.* 3rd Ed. Indianapolis, IN: JIST Publishing, Inc., 2003.

SnagAJob.com. "Working Papers: Everything You Need to Find and Conquer Your First Job." Retrieved on October 18, 2018. http://d1h7kzxfkc767u .cloudfront.net/uploadedfiles/snagajob.com-first-job -guide.pdf.

United States Department of Labor. "Minimum Wage - Wage and Hour Division (WHD) - U.S. Department of Labor." Retrieved on October 18, 2018. http://www .dol.gov/whd/minwage/q-a.htm#full.

U.S. Department of Labor. "Minimum Wage." Retrieved on October 18, 2018. https://www.dol.gov/general /topic/wages/minimumwage.

Weiss, Jodi, and Russell Kahn. *145 Things to Be When You Grow Up: Planning a Successful Career While You're Still in High School.* New York, NY: Princeton Review Publishing, LLC, 2004.

INDEX

ABOUT THE AUTHORS

Xina M. Uhl has authored a variety of books for young people in addition to textbooks, teacher's guides, lessons, and assessment questions. When she is not writing or reading, she enjoys travel, photography, and hiking with her dogs. Her blog features her travel adventures and latest fiction projects.

Daniel E. Harmon was the author of many books and articles for national and regional magazines and newspapers. He wrote numerous books about careers for Rosen Publishing. He lived in Spartanburg, South Carolina.

PHOTO CREDITS